Camping Cookbook For Beginners

Top Tips To Finally Discover How To Prepare Quick, Easy, Delicious And Healthy Recipes On Your Camping Trip With Your Loved Ones

Eddie Hale

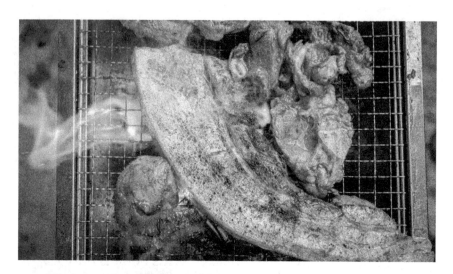

TABLE OF CONTENTS

Introduction

As can be seen from the above descriptions, camping can include so many different activities and there is no single way to describe it. However, what brings together most camping experiences usually involves the wilderness in some capacity, including sleeping outdoors. There are some other terms that may utilize the word "camping" but do not necessarily actually involve setting up tents and sleeping outdoors. This includes longer activities that can be arranged for children or teenagers, such as through a summer camp, where additional facilities may be installed, such as camping halls and bunkhouses. In addition, while homeless people often sleep outdoors, this does not really connote the same idea of camping because it is usually done voluntarily, whereas homelessness has its own problems. In addition, people that live outdoors or have a different kind of lifestyle that involves sleeping outdoors are not considered campers as this can be something particular to their cultures or way of life.

The history of camping can be traced back to Great Britain, whereby a traveler known as Thomas Hiram Holding popularized the term and practice as a recreational pastime. This began taking place more commonly toward the end of the 19th century as a larger number of people began to camp, although they would often use boats to transport their heavy camping equipment. Holding is often credited with popularizing a different kind of camping activity that involved cycling across the country and camping outdoors. He did so in the Americas while traveling with his parents as well as in different parts of Great Britain, such as Ireland. He also wrote a book about his experiences that eventually encouraged people to form groups and similarly cycle and camp across the world. This enabled other people to learn of his experiences and further popularized camping beyond Great Britain as it began being undertaken across the globe, as is additionally described in a second book he wrote in 1908 on the subject matter.

It was in these decades toward the end of the 19th century and the start of the 20th that additional commercial camping grounds were established, including Cunningham's Camp and a camping cite in Weybridge that was set up by the Association of Cycle Campers in 1894 and 1906 respectively. The latter organization eventually expanded to become the National Camping Club and accepted hundreds of members. While camping didn't continue during World War I in the Global North, it was eventually revived later on through the establishment of other forms of camping endeavors, including the Boy Scouts movement. Another actor, William Henry Harrison Murray, is also associated with camping in the US, who also published a book on this topic. Eventually, an international association for camping clubs was established in 1932, which brought together many camping clubs and groups across the world. As such, camping has become a well-loved pastime and frequently practiced venture in the United States and Great Britain, but also elsewhere.

CHAPTER 1: Simple Breakfast Recipes

1. Sweet-n-Savory Pancakes with Bacon:

Serves: 4

Cooking time: 15-30 minutes

Ingredients:

- 8 back bacon rashers

- Olive oil

- ½ teaspoon of salt

- 1 ½ cups of milk

- 1 ¼ cup of flour

- 2½ teaspoons baking powder

- Maple syrup

- 1 whisked egg

- 2 tablespoons vegetable oil

Directions:

1. Place baking powder, salt and flour into a container. Mix together and make a space in the center. Pour the egg, milk, and vegetable oil in and keep whisking an emulsion is formed.

2. Place some oil to heat up in a frying pan. Add approximately 100 ml of the mixture and cook until bubbles appear on the surface. Then, flip the pancake and cook the other side for a few minutes.

3. Place the cooked pancake onto a plate and cover so it remains warm. Repeat this step with the remaining batter, while adding more oil or butter to keep the pan slick.Over a separate pan (or in the same one after the pancakes finish cooking), fry the bacon for 2 minutes on each side or until it begins to sizzle and is completely cooked.

4. Serve the pancakes with bacon and maple syrup.

2. Berry Pancakes with Cream:

Serves: 4

Cooking time: 30 minutes

Ingredients:

- 1 to 2 tablespoons of sugar

- 2 tablespoons of fresh orange juice

- 1 to 2 eggs

- 4 tablespoons of crème fraiche

- 250 g of blueberries or raspberries

- Vegetable oil/butter

- 125 g of flour

Directions:

1. Combine the eggs, milk, and flour in a container and whisk until an emulsion is formed. Set the mixture aside.

2. Over a small flame, place the berries, sugar and orange juice into a small pot. Let the mixture simmer until the berries lose their firmness and the mixture thickens. Take the pot off the flame and let it cool.

3. Place some vegetable oil into a skillet and pour in some batter with a ladle. Wait for the pancake to cook over the flame and flip after the edges turn golden brown. Once the other side is cooked, remove from the flame and place on a serving plate.

4. Prepare the remainder of the pancakes using butter or vegetable oil. If desired, serve the pancakes with crème fraiche and the berry mixture.

3. Muffin-style Frittatas:

Serves: 2

Cooking time: 5 minutes

Ingredients:

- Non-stick cooking spray

- Chopped meat (i.e. ham or sausage)

- Grated cheese (i.e. mozzarella or parmesan)

- 3 large eggs

- 1/4 cup of half and half

- 1/2 teaspoon salt

- Diced onions

- Green peppers

Directions:

1. Combine the salt, half and half, and eggs into a bowl and whisk thoroughly. Then, pour the mixture into different muffin pans in your tin.

2. Place the different toppings you want into each cup, including cheese, peppers, meat, etc. then, place the tin over the fire for 5 minutes or until the eggs are the desired consistency.

3. In order to remove the food from the tin, use a knife to gently loosen it from the container. Serve and consume while warm.

4. Plain Pancakes:

Serves: 4

Cooking time: 20 minutes

Ingredients:

- 1 cup of buttermilk

- ½ teaspoon bicarbonate of soda

- 200 g of flour

- 1 teaspoon baking powder

- 2 eggs, separated whites and yolk

- Vegetable oil

To Serve:

- Marmalade

- Butter

Directions:

1. Crack your eggs and separate the egg whites from the yolks. Take the egg whites and beat them until the peaks begin to stiffen. Then, set aside.

2. Combine the flour, baking soda and baking powder in a bowl and mix. Then, create a small space in the center of the container and place the egg yolks and milk in the center. Mix together thoroughly. Then, fold in the fluffy egg white mixture with a spatula.

3. Place some oil in a skillet and pour some batter into the pan in different scoops (if there is enough space). If there isn't, then just make the pancakes in different stages or steps. While you are waiting for the pancakes to cook, keep an eye out for bubbles forming at the surface or for the edges to brown. Once that happens, flip over the pancake.

4. Once the second side is cooked, take it out of the skillet and put it under a piece of aluminum foil on a plate to stay warm while the other pancakes are cooking. Repeat the abovementioned steps until all the pancakes are done. Use additional oil if needed to prevent the pancakes from sticking to the pan.

5. Serve with butter and jam while warm.

5. Hot Cereal:

Serves: 4

Cooking time: 5 minutes

Ingredients:

- 1 cup of whole wheat flakes

- 1 cup of oats

- 1 cup of ground flaxseed

- 1 cup of seven-grain cereal

- 1 cup of bran

Directions:

1. To prepare, combine the cereal with the water and bring to a boil in a pan. Then, once it boils, reduce the heat and allow the mixture to simmer for 5 minutes or until it reaches the desired consistency.

2. Remove the pan from the flame and pour into a bowl. Allow it to cool before eating.

6. French Toast:

Serves: 2-4

Cooking time: 4 minutes

Ingredients:

- Oil or nonstick cooking spray

- 4 small eggs

- 7 slices of toast

- 1 teaspoon ground cinnamon

- 1/3 cup of milk

Directions:

1. Place some oil on a frying pan. As it heats up, combine the cinnamon, eggs, and milk together and beat until they form an emulsion. Then, soak a slice of toast thoroughly in the mixture before placing it on the heated pan.

2. Cook the piece until the edges of the bread turn brown and then flip and allow the other side to cook evenly for about 2 to 3 minutes. Repeat this step for the next pieces of bread and add additional oil or cooking spray as needed.

3. Place the French toast on a plate and cover so it remains warm.

4. Serve with toppings such as icing sugar, strawberries or maple syrup.

7. Fragrant Banana Pancakes:

Serves: 4

Cooking time: 10-15 minutes

Ingredients:

- 2 teaspoons cardamom seed powder

- 300 g of self-rising flour

- 3 large ripe bananas

- 1 egg, whisked

- Honey (optional)

- Vegetable oil

- ½ cup of milk

- 2 tablespoons of sugar

- 2 tablespoons vegetable oil

Directions:

1. In a large container, combine all the wet and dry ingredients (with the exception of the honey and cooking spray) and mix well together until an emulsion is formed.

2. Place some oil in a skillet and wait for it to heat up over a medium-high flame. Then, pour half a cup of the batter into the frying pan and wait until the pancake cooks (about 2 to 4 minutes). Flip over once the edges turn golden brown and the pancake is thoroughly cooked. Then, take the pancake off the pan and repeat this step until all the batter is finished. Use more oil as is needed.

3. Serve the pancakes with honey, if desired.

8. Basic Burritos:

Serves: 4

Cooking time: 5 minutes

Ingredients:

- Picante

- Salt and pepper

- 1/2 cup of grated mozzarella or parmesan

- 1/2 cup of milk or water

- 1 small diced onion

- 5 large eggs

- 7 tortillas

- 1 tablespoon butter

Directions:

1. Mix the pepper, salt, eggs and milk together in a large bowl. Then, add some butter to a frying pan. Wait for

it to heat up. Then, sauté the onions in the butter for a few minutes until they become translucent

2. Pour in the egg mixture and cook over a medium-high flame, while stirring to prevent the food from sticking to the bottom.

3. Warm up your tortillas and place the cheese in them so that it can melt a bit. Then, place the eggs in the tortillas and roll it up to create a wrap.

4. Serve while warm.

9. Raisin-bread French Toast:

Serves: 4

Cooking time: 10 minutes

Ingredients:

- Sour cream (optional)

- 2 tablespoons butter

- ¼ teaspoon ground cinnamon

- 2 oranges

- 2 tablespoons vegetable oil

- 6 slices of raisin bread

- 3 to 4 tablespoons of milk

- 3 small eggs

Directions:

1. Zest your oranges and put the rind aside. Then, remove the orange seeds and the inner and outer skin

of the orange and separate the oranges into different

pieces.

2. Take the pieces of bread and cut it into diagonal slices.

Then, whisk the cinnamon, milk and eggs together in

a small bowl.

3. Place half the oil and butter into a skillet and wait until

it heats up. Then, pour in the egg mixture and

immediately place the pieces of bread into the mix.

Quickly flip them so that both sides of each piece is

coating the egg mixture. Then, once the sides of the

egg are cooked, which should take about 5 minutes,

flip the egg upside down so the other side gets cooked

and turns brown. Remove from the pan and leave it

covered so it stays warm. Then, repeat with the

leftover bread and egg mixture.

4. Place some of the orange zest and sour cream (if

desired) on the bread and serve.

10. Marinated Cheese Casserole:

Serves: 4

Cooking time: 35 minutes

Ingredients:

- 3 cups of grated cheese (i.e. mozzarella or parmesan)

- 1/2 chopped medium onion

- 1 diced sun-dried tomato

- 2 cups of milk

- 5 large eggs, whisked

- Salt and pepper

- 7 thin slices of toast

Directions:

1. After buttering up the sides of a metal tin, put a few pieces of bread side by side in the bottom of the dish. Layer this with half of the cheese.

2. Separately, combine the eggs, tomatoes, milk, and onions in a dish and whisk together. Then, pour this mixture into the tin and top it off with the remaining cheese. Add salt and pepper to taste.

3. Cover the tin and place into the fridge or cooler to marinate overnight.

4. The next day, pre-heat in a Dutch oven at 350° for approximately 30 to 40 minutes or until it is fully cooked. Once you take it out of the oven, let it rest for 7 to 10 minutes.

5. Then, cut into pieces and serve while still warm.

11. Caramel French Toast:

Serves: 2

Cooking time: 15-20 minutes

Ingredients:

- 1 large banana, sliced into thin pieces

- 1 teaspoon of vegetable oil

- 1 tablespoon of sugar

- 3 tablespoons of caramel sauce

- 1 egg

- 2 tablespoons of unsalted butter

- 2 thick slices of bread

- 15 g of roughly chopped pecan nuts

- ¼ teaspoon ground cinnamon

- 2 to 3 tablespoons milk

Directions:

1. Beat an egg in a bowl. Then, move to a shallow dish and whisk in sugar, cinnamon and milk. Then, take the bread slices and place them in the mixture for a few seconds before flipping them upside down until they have absorbed the batter on both sides.

2. Heat the oil and butter in a skillet and then add the bread and cook until the sides turn golden brown. Then, flip it over and wait until it gets fully cooked. Remove from the heat and put it in a dish.

3. Remove any excess oil and toast the pecan nuts in the pan, while tossing occasionally. Add caramel sauce and the banana. Then, spoon onto the French toast and serve warm.

CHAPTER 2: Campfire Barbeque-Style Meals

12. Lean Steaks with Green Beans

Serves: 4

Cooking time: 5 minutes

Ingredients:

- Salt and pepper

- 400 g of green beans

- 200 g of arugula

- 1 teaspoon olive oil

- 4 thin steaks

- Crusty bread, to serve

Tomato dressing

- 2 diced tomatoes

- 1 tablespoon of mustard

- 1 diced shallot

- 1 to 2 teaspoons of olive oil

- 1 tablespoon red wine vinegar

Directions:

1. Place some water in a pot to boil and salt it. Then, add green beans and cook them for 2 to 3 minutes so that they soften but do not lose their shape. Once they are done, drain them.

2. Combine the remaining ingredients together in a bowl to prepare the tomato mixture.

3. In the meantime, combine all the ingredients in a big bowl together to make the tomato sauce. Add the drained beans and sprinkle some salt and pepper on them. Then, mix together and cover so it can stay warm.

4. Place some oil on the steaks and sear for 1 minute on both sides on a very hot grill or barbecue pit. Cook

longer if you want your steaks to be more well-done. Then, remove from the heat and set aside so it can cool.

5. Place the arugula into four different bowls. Then, add the sauce and beans to the tops of the salads as well as the steaks lastly.

6. Divide the rocket salad into bowls andplace over the sauce and beans, then top with the steaks. Serve with crusty bread.

13.Spicy Thai Beef Patties

Serves: 4

Cooking time: 10 minutes

Ingredients:

- Cup of shredded lettuce

- Olive oil, for brushing

- Sweet chili sauce

- 1 baguette, cut into four pieces

Burger mix

- 2 tablespoons fresh coriander (finely chopped)

- 1 tablespoon light soy sauce

- 1 egg, whisked

- Pepper

- 1 tablespoon Thai red curry paste

- 500 g of minced beef

- 25 g of fresh white breadcrumbs

Directions:

1. Combine the minced beef and breadcrumbs, egg, pepper, red curry paste, coriander, and soy sauce in a bowl with your hands. Separate the mixture into high different balls and then flatten them to create burgers.

2. Apply some oil to each burger and place over a campfire or grill for 4-5 minutes on each side. If the burgers need more or less time than this, adjust this time accordingly.

3. Place each burger in the buns and serve with the sweet chili sauce and shredded lettuce.

14. American Hamburger

Serves: 4

Cooking time: 10-12 minutes

Ingredients:

- Cup of shredded lettuce

- 2 tablespoons mustard

- 1 large onion (cut into ringlets)

- Ketchup

- 3 medium-sized tomatoes, sliced

- 4 burger buns

- Olive oil, for brushing

- 2 to 3 dill pickles, cut into thin slices

Burger mix

- 1 teaspoon Worcestershire sauce

- 250 g of minced pork belly

- 500 g of minced rib-eye steak

- 1 tablespoon of drained capers

- Salt and pepper

- 1 finely chopped onion

Directions: Place the onions, capers, Worcestershire sauce, salt, pepper, minced beef and pork into a container. Mix them thoroughly together using your hands and create four round beef patties. Cover the burgers and refrigerate or store in a cooler for 30 minutes.Place some oil on the burgers and grill over a fire for 4 to 6 minutes or until the burger is sufficiently cooked through. As you wait for the burger patties to cook, toast the burger buns simultaneously on the grill.Apply mustard and ketchup to the tops and bottoms of the buns (based on individual preference). Then, add the burgers, shredded lettuce, pickles, tomato slices, and thin onion rings. Serve while the patties are still warm.

15.Flavorful Steaks with Cherry Tomatoes

Serves: 4 **Cooking time:** 10 minutes

Ingredients:

- 4 lean fillet steaks 8 cherry tomatoes, halved

- 1 tablespoon green peppercorns in brine, drained

- 1 teaspoon balsamic vinegar

- 2 tablespoons light soy sauce

Directions : Place a pan over a grill stand and wait for it to become extremely hot. Then, sear the stakes on the griddle tray for a few minutes on each side, roughly 2 to 5 minutes, and then place on a dish. Cover it and allow it to cool as any remaining steaks cook.Prepare the sauce by pouring the balsamic vinegar and soy sauce into the tray, further adding the cherry tomatoes and peppercorns. Allow it to cook until the cherry tomatoes soften and the sauce thickens slightly. Then, serve the sauce with the steaks.

16.Garlicky Lamb Leg with Yogurt Dip

Serves: 6

Cooking time: 30-40 minutes

Ingredients:

- 2 tablespoons olive oil

- 5 to 6 minced garlic cloves

- 3 tablespoons green peppercorns in brine, drained and crushed

- 4 handfuls of chopped parsley

- 1 butterflied leg of lamb, about 1.5 to 2 kg

- 3 handfuls of mint leaves

Broad bean and dill yogurt

- Salt

- ¼ cup chopped dill

- 100 g of small broad beans

- ¾ cup of Greek yogurt

Directions:

1. Combine the oil, parsley, garlic, mint, and peppercorns together. Put the lamb in a non-metallic dish and split open. Rub the garlic mixture into the meat and cover the container. Leave it to marinate in the fridge overnight or in a cooler for a few hours at least.

2. After preparing the campfire or barbecue area, place the lamb on a grill rack and barbecue until pink in the center and browned on the outside, which should take approximately 20 minutes. Once done, place on a plate and let it rest for 15 minutes so it can remain juicy.

3. Separately, prepare the yogurt mix by boiling the beans in a pot of water for up to 5 minutes. Once they are soft, drain them and allow them to cool. Then,

remove the outer layer of the beans and place in a bowl. Then, combine with milk, salt, and dill and place in a dish.

4. Serve the meat with the yogurt dip.

17. Aromatic Marinated Steak

Serves: 4-5 **Cooking time:** 30 minutes

Ingredients:

- ½ teaspoon black pepper powder

- 8 juniper berries

- Salt

- 2 tablespoons of Worcestershire sauce

- 600 g piece of steak

- 1 tablespoon mustard

- 2 tablespoons sugar

- 2 tablespoons whisky

- 2 to 3 tablespoons black treacle

Directions:

1. Crush the juniper berries with a mortar and pestle. Then, combine with Worcestershire sauce, whiskey,

pepper, sugar, mustard, and treacle and mix thoroughly. Then, place the stick in a glass container and rub the marinade into it. Cover the container and store in an ice box for an hour or two.

2. After the hour is up, place the steak in a plate and sprinkle some salt on each side. Then, move to a grill rack over a campfire and grill for about 15 minutes on each side. In order to test if the meat is well done, use a meat thermometer. It should be around 160 to 165°F if it is fully cooked through.

3. Place the remaining marinade juices into a skillet and heat as the steak continues to be grilled. Once the meat is fully done, move it to the side and allow it to rest for ten minutes. Then, cut it into thinner slices and serve with the marinade juices.

18.Minced Lamb and Feta Salad

Serves: 4 **Cooking time:** 8-10 minutes

Ingredients:

- Crusty bread (optional)

- Salt and pepper

- 2 to 3 tablespoons olive oil

- 1 tablespoon chopped rosemary

- Grated rind of 1 lemon

- 2 tablespoons of chopped oregano

- 500 g of minced lamb

Feta Salad

- 1 tablespoon chopped oregano

- ½ small red onion (diced)

- Grated lemon rind 1 lemon (juice)

- 2 tablespoons of chopped parsley

- 200 g of feta cheese, sliced

- 3 tablespoons olive oil

Directions:

1. Combine the salt, pepper, lemon zest, oil, and spices together in a glass container. Mix properly with the minced lamb. Then, form three to four long kebabs and place a metal skewer through each piece.Grill the lamb kebabs for between 5 and 8 minutes on a hot grill rack. Remember to rotate so that each side of the kebabs cook evenly. Once they're done, remove from the heat and set aside so that they can cool.Separately, take the sliced pieces of feta cheese and combine with the chopped onion, spices, lemon zest, olive oil, and lemon juice. Mix evenly and add salt and pepper to taste.

2. Serve the feta salad and lamb together with bread and any juices from the griddle tray.

19.Anchovy-Flavored Lamb Kebabs with Olive Salad

Serves: 4 **Cooking time:** 7-10 minutes

Ingredients:

- Salt and pepper

- Olive oil

- 1 tablespoon chopped rosemary

- 500 g of minced lamb

- 1 minced garlic clove

- 1 small onion (diced)

- 4 to 6 anchovies (drained and chopped)

Tomato and olive salad

- 1 red onion, diced

- 2 tablespoons olive oil

- A few basil leaves

- 125 g of pitted black olives

- 6 tomatoes, cut into wedges

- Squeeze of lemon juice

Directions:

1. Using your hands, combine the anchovies, rosemary, beef, salt, pepper, garlic, diced onion in a large bowl. Separate the mixture into 12 even balls and mold into sausage shapes. Leave the sausages to rest for 30 minutes in a cooler or in a refrigerator.Take each sausage and place a metal skewer through it, across its length. Brush some oil across piece and grill for 4 to 5 minutes across a grill rack or fire pit until cooked evenly. Remember to rotate the skewers. Separately, combine the basil, tomatoes, salt, onion, olives and pepper in a bowl. Add a drizzle of olive oil and some lemon juice and then mix evenly.

2. Serve the kebabs with the salad.

20.Grilled Pork Ribs

Serves: 4

Cooking time: 20-40 minutes

Ingredients:

- 1 tablespoon dark soy sauce

- Salt and pepper

- 4 x 500 g packs of pork spare ribs

- 1 tablespoon olive oil

- 1 tablespoon malt vinegar

- 2 tablespoons of honey

- 100 ml of tomato ketchup

- 2 teaspoons mustard (preferably Dijon)

Directions:

1. Combine all the ingredients with the exception of the pork spare ribs. Then, after having formed the

marinade, apply it to the meat with a brush so that it is evenly coated.

2. Place the ribs on a pre-heated grill rack over a barbecue for 25 to 30 minutes or until it is evenly cooked. Make sure to rotate the meat so that it doesn't overcook or get burned on one side.

3. Allow it to rest for a few minutes and then serve immediately.

21. Spicy Lamb Chops

Serves: 4 **Cooking time:** 10-15 minutes

Ingredients:

- 2 teaspoons of muscovite sugar

- 4 lamb chops

- 2 to 3 green chilies, deseeded and thinly sliced

- 2 tablespoons of sherry

- 2 to 3 minced garlic cloves

- 2 to 3 cm piece of fresh ginger, peeled and grated

- Fire-baked potatoes, to serve

- 3 tablespoons soy sauce

Directions:

1. Combine the sherry, ginger, sugar, soy sauce, chili and garlic in a glass dish. Then, pour this mixture over the lamb chops

2. Refrigerate the meat overnight or for at least 2 to 3 hours so that it can marinate and become tender.

3. Afterward, place the lamb chops on a grill rack over a barbecue pit or campfire and grill for 5 to 8 minutes or until it is cooked according to taste.

4. Serve with some pre-prepared baked potatoes.

22. Lemony Pork Schnitzel

Serves: 4

Cooking time: 5 minutes

Ingredients:

- 1 tablespoon chopped parsley

- 4 trimmed pork schnitzels, 125 g each

- 4–6 tablespoons lemon juice

- Salt and pepper

- 1 tablespoon drained and chopped capers

- 5 tablespoons of olive oil

- 3 tablespoons chopped mint

Directions:

1. Mix the oil, spices, capers, oil and lemon juice together in a container.

2. Brush the pork with some oil and place some salt and pepper on each salt. Then, grill for 2 to 5 minutes on a grill rack or until cooked evenly across both sides.

3. Then, serve with the lemon and caper sauce.

23. Chorizo Pizzas with Quail Eggs

Serves: 2

Cooking time: 30 minutes

Ingredients:

- 150 g of flour

- ½ teaspoon salt

- ½ teaspoon of dried yeast

- 1 tablespoon olive oil

Topping

- Tablespoons olive oil

- 1 minced garlic clove

- Arugula (optional)

- 100 g of grated Manchego cheese

- 1 deseeded and halved green chili

- 100 grams of chorizo sausage (thinly sliced)

- Salt and pepper

- 6 quail eggs

- 1 to 2 tablespoons of pine nuts

Directions:

1. In a large bowl, mix the salt, yeast, flour and olive oil to create the pizza base. Once this is mixed together, pour in hot water slowly and continue mixing until the dough is complete. Add a little bit of water or flour, depending on if the dough is too dry or too moist until you have achieved a dough-like consistency. Continue kneading for approximately 10 minutes in the bowl or across a flat surface. Then, allow the dough to rise for 30 minutes and cover with a clean cloth or plastic wrap. Before using, the dough should have doubled in size.

2. In order to make the pizza, take out a durable baking sheet or a pizza paddle. In a separate bowl, mix the garlic and olive oil. Set this aside.

3. Take the dough out of the bowl and split it in two. Then, roll one of the pieces out onto a floured board. Using a rolling pin, create a large circular shape that can sufficiently fit onto your pizza spatula. Grab your baking sheet and some garlic oil to it before placing the pizza dough on it. Then, take your cut up sausage and spread half of it across the pizza. Similarly, scatter half the chili and add the desired toppings onto the pizzas, including the cheese, pine nuts, and eggs (which should be placed into small wells on the pizza's surfaces). Add salt and pepper to taste. Repeat this step with the second piece of dough.

4. Cover the pizzas with aluminum foil and tuck under the based to cover them so that no coal gets onto the pizzas as they cook, which should take about 30 minutes. Rotate the pizzas on the rack. After the pizzas are fully cooked, serve with arugula if desired.

24. Pork Chops With Spicy Corn

Serves: 4

Cooking time: 10-20 minutes

Ingredients:

- 1 diced red chili

- 3 spring onions, thinly sliced

- 1 cup of finely chopped coriander leaves

- ¾ cup of sweet corn kernels

- 4 pork chops

- 5 tablespoons of crème fraiche

- 2 tablespoons olive oil

- Salt and pepper

- Lime zest

Directions:

1. Apply some oil to the chops using a brush and dust lightly with some salt and pepper. Then, grill over a barbecue or campfire for approximately 10 minutes (or less if it cooks more quickly). Set it aside to rest for a few minutes.

2. Separately, heat the remaining oil in a skillet and add the corn. Sauté for about 2 minutes and then add the chili and spring onions for another minute.

3. Lastly, pour in the crème fraiche while stirring continuously. Further add the lemon zest, salt and pepper. Lastly, sprinkle the finely chopped coriander leaves across the meat and serve.

CHAPTER 3: Lunches & Snacks

25.Sautéed Liver and Bacon

Serves: 4 **Cooking time:** 10 minutes

Ingredients:

- 8 strips of bacon 1 tablespoon olive oil

- 150 ml dry cider

- Salt and pepper

- 625g of calf's liver

- 2 tablespoons vegetable oil

- Flour (to coat)

- 1 handful of large sage leaves

Directions:

1. In a separate container, mix the salt, pepper and flour together. Take some of this flour and apply it to the liver.

2. Then, in a skillet, heat the vegetable oil and lightly sauté the sage leaves for about 25 seconds. Then, remove them and add the bacon to the pan. Fry it until it is brown and then remove from the pan.

3. Then, fry the liver for about 2 minutes or until it turns golden. Then, add the bacon and sage to the pan and cook for another 2 minutes combined. Remove everything from the pan at this stage.

4. Pour some cider into the pan and allow it to steam and reduce in volume. Then, add any other butter and re-season if needed. Place the sage leaves, liver and bacon in a plate and spoon some of the sauce on top of them. Serve hot.

26. Simple Fried Rice:

Serves: 3

Cooking time: 5 minutes

Ingredients:

- Salt and pepper

- 1 cup of cold pre-boiled rice

- Hot sauce

- 1/4 cup of milk

- 4 eggs

- 1 tablespoon vegetable oil

Directions:

Heat some butter in a nonstick pan or wok. Then, fry the eggs

quickly and set aside. Then, re-add the eggs, hot sauce, milk,

salt, pepper and pre-boiled rice. Mix thoroughly and serve.

27. Campfire-Friendly Popcorn:

Serves: 2

Cooking time: 5 minutes

Ingredients:

- 4 tablespoons popcorn kernels

- 3 tablespoons of canola oil

- Salt

Directions

Tear two large pieces of aluminum foil that are of roughly the same size and join them together to create a pocket. Insert some popcorn kernels into this pocket and seal it so that there is enough space for the popcorn to pop. Then, place it over the fire and wait for the kernels to pop. Once you can no longer hear the popping sound, remove the bag from the fire. Season with salt and serve immediately.

28. Cannellini Beans with Bacon and Liver

Serves: 4

Cooking time: 10 minutes

Ingredients:

- 3 tablespoons crème fraiche

- 4 tablespoons flour

- 4 large leeks, sliced

- Chopped parsley or thyme (to garnish)

- 4 teaspoons olive oil

- 500 g of canned beans (i.e. cannellini), drained

- 4 bacon rashers, chopped into small pieces

- Salt and pepper

- 4 125g pieces of calf liver

Directions:

1. Combine some flour with salt and pepper. Coat the liver in this mixture and then drop into a pre-heated pan.

2. Fry the liver for minutes on each side, which is usually until it turns pink in the center. Otherwise, you may fry it longer if you want it to be crispier. Then, remove the liver from the pan.

3. Add the remaining oil to the pan and sauté the leeks and bacon until they are thoroughly cooked. Then, mix in the cannellini beans and crème fraiche. Add salt and pepper.

4. Serve the liver with the beans and any other herb as garnish.

29. Raisin Muffins:

Serves: 12

Cooking time: 18 min

Ingredients:

- 1/2 cup of raisins

- 2 teaspoons baking powder

- 1/2 cup of sugar

- 2 eggs, whisked

- 2 cups buttermilk

- 3/4 cup of butter

- 1/4 cup honey

- 1 pinch of salt

- 1 ½ cup of bran

- 2 teaspoons baking soda

- 1 1/4 cup flour

- 1 ½ cup of flour

Directions:

1. Combine all the liquid ingredients together. If you have a liquid mixture that is already frozen, make sure to thaw it so that it reaches room temperature.

2. Pre-heat a Dutch oven to 400 °F. Then, combine the wet and dry ingredients together to form a batter.

3. Once it is smooth, ladle some of the batter into the cups of a muffin tin.

4. Cook the muffins for 15 to 25 minutes, checking to see if the muffins are browned. To be sure, insert a toothpick into the muffins and if it comes back clean, they should be fully baked.

30. Pork Sausage and Sweet Potato

Serves: 4 **Cooking time:** 45 minutes

Ingredients:

- 7 sage leaves

- Salt and pepper

- 2 tablespoons balsamic vinegar

- 4 red onions, thinly sliced

- 6 large pork sausages

- 1 teaspoon sugar

- 500 g of sweet potatoes, cut into small pieces

- 2 to 3 tablespoons olive oil

Directions:

1. Place some oil in a pan and sauté the sausages for 10 minutes until they begin to brown. Then, remove from the pan and place in a dish.

2. Put the onions and sugar in a pan and allow them to brown, mixing frequently. Then, add a bit of salt, the sweet potatoes, pepper and sage leaves and stir. Add the sausages again to the pan.

3. Seal the pan with a lid and allow the mixture to simmer for 25 minutes, at least until the potatoes soften and all the contents are fully cooked. Add some vinegar as well as salt, pepper and additional spices if needed.

4. Serve while hot.

31. Lamb with Eggplant and Dates

Serves: 6

Cooking time: 1 hour 30 minutes

Ingredients:

- 1 teaspoon rosewater

- Salt and pepper

- 1 handful of roughly chopped pitted dates

- 5 tablespoons olive oil

- 350 g couscous

- 2 eggplants, cut into small pieces

- 350 ml chicken stock

- 4 minced garlic cloves

- 1 teaspoon each of ground turmeric, cinnamon, cumin and coriander

- 400 g can of chopped tomatoes

- 2 eggplants

- ½ teaspoon ground cloves

- 2 chopped red onions

- ½ inch piece of peeled and grated fresh ginger

- 1 kg of lean lamb meat, cut into small chunks

Directions:

1. Place some olive oil in a skillet and sauté the eggplants for 10 minutes until they turn golden brown. Keep stirring to prevent them from sticking to the bottom. Then, move to another plate.

2. In the same pan, fry the lamb meat until it turns brown. If the meat cannot fit into the pan, cook it in different portions. Then, add the onions and cook everything for a few more minutes, while further adding any spices and garlic.

3. Then, add the stock and leave the food to simmer for an hour while it is covered or at least until the meat

becomes tender. Next, add the rosewater, eggplants and dates and allow the entire mixture to stay on the heat for 20 more minutes. Make sure to stir on occasion.

4. Grab a glass bowl or a heat-resistant container and pour the couscous into the bowl. Then, pour 450 ml of boiling water over the couscous. Cover it and allow it to sit for a few minutes before fluffing it with a fork.

5. Plate the lamb and add some salt and pepper to taste, which should be consumed with the couscous.

32. Corn and Black-eyed Pea Mix:

Serves: 3

Cooking time: None

Ingredients:

- 2/3 cups chopped cilantro

- 1 can of black-eyed peas

- ¼ chopped green pepper

- 1 can drained black beans

- 1 to 3 diced jalapenos (to taste)

- 7 scallion stalks, chopped

- 2 cans of corn

- Tortilla chips

Dressing:

- A generous pinch of salt

- A small pinch of pepper

- 3 minced garlic cloves

- ¼ cup olive oil

- ¼ cup red wine vinegar

- 1 teaspoon cumin

Directions:

Combine all the main ingredients together, with the exception of tortilla chips. Then, put all the ingredients for the dressing together. Apply the dressing to the corn and black-eyed pea mix. The tortilla chips should then be served with the prepped food.

33. Roasted Hot Dogs:

Serves: 3-6

Cooking time: 5 minutes

Ingredients:

- 1 can of crescent rolls

- 6 hot dogs

Directions:

1. Open the crescent roll can and take out the dough. Cut up the dough in the shape that is desired, with enough surface area to cover each hot dog individually. Then, place each hot dog in the middle of the dough and wrap it up. Then, place the hot dogs on the grill stand over the barbecue or campfire. Wait until the hot dogs and the dough are fully cooked before serving.

34. Quick Cassoulet

Serves: 4

Cooking time: 30 minutes

Ingredients:

- 2 cans of drained cannellini beans

- Salt and pepper

- 2 teaspoons smoked paprika

- 2 tablespoons chopped parsley

- 2 small onions, chopped

- 2 celery stalks, chopped into thin slices

- 2 cans of flavored, chopped tomatoes

- 2 tablespoons olive oil

- 4 boneless, skinless chicken thighs

- 5 sausages

Directions:

1. Heat up some oil in a skillet and sauté the chicken thighs and sausages for 5 minutes until they turn a golden brown. Make sure to stir so that they don't stick to the bottom of the pan. Then, remove the meat from the pan.

2. Add the celery and onion to the skillet and sauté for a few minutes until they soften, which should be 3 to 5 minutes. Then, add the paprika and mix thoroughly, while further placing the meat back into the pan.

3. Insert the tomatoes and beans in the sauce, while further adding salt and pepper if needed. While covering the pan, allow the mixture to simmer until everything is fully cooked. Then, serve with a bit of garnish (i.e. parsley).

35. Pork Goulash with Dumplings

Serves: 6

Cooking time: 2 hours 30 minutes

Ingredients:

- 750 ml hot pork or chicken stock

- 3 tablespoons light muscovite sugar

- ½ kg of red cabbage, shredded

- 4 tablespoons tomato purée

- 1 tablespoon paprika

- 2 tablespoons red wine vinegar

- 2 red onions, sliced

- 2 tablespoons vegetable oil

- Salt and pepper

- 1 kg of lean minced pork

Dumplings

- 100g beef or vegetable suet

- 1 teaspoon caraway seeds

- 150g of self-rising flour

Directions:

1. Heat a large pan and add some oil. Once hot, place the pork in the oil and allow it to brown, before removing it from the pan. Then, fry some onions and add the meat again, stirring them together for the next few minutes.

2. Next, add the sugar, tomato purée, vinegar, stock, sugar and paprika and stir everything together. Allow the mixture to boil and then cover with a lid. Reduce the heat and allow the mixture to simmer for 60 to 75 minutes.

3. Afterward, add the cabbage to the dish and allow it to simmer for 15 more minutes or until it softens.

4. In a separate glass bowl, blend the suet, caraway seeds, and rice together, further adding salt and pepper to taste. To thicken the mixture, add cold water and keep whisking until it reaches the desired consistency.

5. Add some hot water to the goulash if the stock has been reduced extensively as the dumplings will likely have absorbed some of the stock. Then, cover the lid of the pot and cook until the dumplings are ready, which should be up to 15 minutes. Serve immediately.

36. Arugula Pasta with Sausage

Serves: 4

Cooking time: 15 minutes

Ingredients:

- 1 teaspoon chili flakes

- 7 skinless sausages, chopped into thin slices

- 2 to 3 cups of arugula

- Salt and pepper

- 2 tablespoons olive oil

- 450g pasta

To serve

- ready-cooked penne or other pasta

- grated Parmesan cheese

Directions:

1. Heat some oil in a skillet and sauté the sausages for a few minutes, stirring occasionally until they darken. Then, add some pasta, chili, pepper and salt. Cover the mixture and allow the sauce to reduce and the meat to cook evenly.

2. Combine the spaghetti with the arugula and mix them all together. Serve while hot.

37. Chunky Chorizo Stew

Serves: 4

Cooking time: 40 minutes

Ingredients:

- 2 tablespoons chopped thyme

- 4 tablespoons chopped basil

- Salt and pepper

- Grated parmesan cheese

- 2 cans of drained borlotti beans

- 250 grams of pasta shapes (i.e. conchigliette)

- ¾ liter of hot beef stock

- 3 tablespoons olive oil

- 500 to 750g of pasta

- 4 minced garlic cloves

- 2 small chorizo sausages, chopped

- 1 diced large onion

Directions:

1. In a large saucepan, add some oil and sauté some onions, garlic, thyme and sausages for a few minutes until the meat is cooked and the onions have softened.

2. Then, place some borlotti beans, stock, pasta, salt and pepper in a pot and bring it to a boil. Then, reduce the heat and allow it to simmer for 20 minutes while covered. Lastly, drain the water and add the meat to the pasta and bean mix.

3. Add the basil and mix well. Then, taste the food to see if additional seasoning is needed.

4. Serve with grated Parmesan cheese.

38. Sausage with Lentils

Serves: 4

Cooking time: 40 minutes

Ingredients:

- Crusty bread

- 125 ml fruity red wine

- Chopped parsley, to garnish

- 150g red legumes

- 250g of chorizo sausage, thickly sliced

- 1 tablespoon olive oil

- 500 ml warmed chicken stock

- ½ large onion, diced

Directions:

1. Heat up some oil in a pan and fry the chorizo for 1 to 2 minutes before removing from the pan to a plate.

2. Next, add the onion to the pan and cook until it becomes translucent, for about three minutes. Then, pour in the wine and the lentils. Increase the heat to bring the mixture to a boil and then reduce it and allow the food to simmer for 20 to 30 minutes.

3. Once most of the sauce has evaporated and the lentils have become tender, add the warmed chicken stock and the meat to the dish and allow it to simmer.

4. Serve with finely chopped parsley and bread.

39. Bruschetta with Cilantro and Tomato:

Serves: 4

Cooking time: 5-10 minutes

Ingredients:

- 1 rough-chopped large tomato

- 1 small red onion, diced

- 1 teaspoon balsamic vinegar

- 1 baguette, sliced into thick pieces

- 1 cup of chopped cilantro leaves

- 2 tablespoons olive oil

- Salt and pepper to taste

- 1 minced garlic clove

Directions:

1. Combine the cilantro, onion, garlic, tomatoes, pepper, garlic, olive oil, vinegar and salt in a small bowl. Then,

separately toast some bread and drizzle some olive oil onto it.

2. Serve with bread with the tomato mixture on top.

40. Cheesy Nachos:

Serves: 6

Cooking time: 10 minutes

Ingredients:

- 2 cups of grated cheddar cheese

- 1/2 cup salsa

- 2 medium-sized bags of nacho chips

Directions:

1. Pour the nachos onto a big metal pan and spread out the cheese and salsa on top of it. Place the tin over an open fire to enable the cheese to melt a bit. Be careful not to get burned, however.

CHAPTER 4: Evening Meals

41.Rib-Eye Steak with Asparagus

Serves: 2

Cooking time: 10 minutes

Ingredients:

- Salt and black pepper

- 2 rib-eye steaks (with bone)

- 450g asparagus, tough ends removed

- Juice of one lemon

- Vegetable oil

- 5 tablespoons olive oil

Directions:

1. Rub some salt and pepper into the rib-eye steaks and leave them for a few minutes.

2. Take a dish and place your asparagus stalks on it. Then, drizzle with olive oil and lemon juice, while further adding salt and pepper.

3. Once the barbecue or grill area is ready, add some oil to the grater and sear the stakes for 3 to 5 minutes on each side.

4. Next to the steaks, place the asparagus on the grill and cook them for five minutes in total, while rotating occasionally to ensure each side of the stalks gets roasted.

5. Serve the steaks with asparagus.

42. Zesty Fish Fillets:

Serves: 2 **Cooking time:** 10 minutes

Ingredients:

- Juice of one lemon

- Pinch of salt and pepper

- Sunflower oil

- Grated lemon rind

- 4 scallions

- 2 boneless fish fillets

- 1 crushed garlic clove

- 5 sprigs of dill

- 2 tablespoons of olive oil

Directions:

1. If you have lime souse that is frozen, make sure to defrost it before use.

2. Take your boneless fish fillets and pat them dry to remove any excess moisture. Then, place some scallions and dill along the fillet. Repeat this step with the other fillet and cover each while further coating them with some oil. Wrap each of the fillets in aluminum foil.

3. Place the two fillets on a grill stand for about 10 minutes until the fish meat turns white and can be easily flaked with a fork. Add salt and pepper to taste and serve with the lime sauce.

43.Pizza with Beer Crust:

Serves: 6

Cooking time: 20 minutes

Ingredients:

Crust:

- 1 tablespoon dried oregano or basil

- 3 cups of flour

- Generous pinch of salt

- 1 tablespoon baking powder

- 1 350 ml can of beer

Pizza Filling:

- Generous pinch of dried oregano

- 3 small garlic cloves, minced

- Salt and pepper to taste

- ½ cup shredded parmesan cheese

- 1 ½ cup shredded mozzarella cheese

- 1 tablespoon dried basil

- 3 large chopped tomatoes

Toppings: (based on preference)

- Chopped onion

- Pineapple

- Black pitted olives

- Chopped bell pepper

- Pepperoni

- Mushrooms

Directions:

1. Mix the beer and flour in a large pot and begin knead with your hands on a flat surface until the dough reaches the desired consistency. Then, spread it out with a rolling pin and split it to fit into two pizza pans.

2. Brush the dough on each pan with some oil and further spread out the sliced tomatoes, basil, cheeses, and other toppings. Ensure that the dough is properly spread out in each of the two pizza pans.

3. Bake the pizzas on a grill rack until the dough is properly cooked. Then, using a pizza cutter or a knife, cut into pieces and serve.

44.Pineapple-Flavored Pork Chops:

Serves: 4 **Cooking time:** 12 minutes

Ingredients:

- 1 tablespoon sesame oil 1 small onion, diced

- 2 tablespoons sugar (brown or white)

- Bone-on pork chops 1 cup pineapple juice

- 3 tablespoons soy sauce Salt and black pepper

Directions:

1. Combine all the ingredients together with the exception of the meat to form the marinade. Apply this to the pork chops and then place the meat on an oiled grill rack over a flame and allow it to cook for 7 minutes or so on each side. To ensure the meat is fully cooked, check the temperature using a meat thermometer as it should reach 170 ° F closer to the bone.

45. Beef or Chicken Corn Dogs

Serves: 8 **Cooking time:** 30 minutes

Ingredients:

- 8 beef or chicken hot dogs 8 slices cheddar cheese

- 2 quartered pickles 1 package biscuit dough

- Disposable wooden sticks

Directions:

1. Insert a disposable wooden stick into each hotdog and then lightly grill over a fire to partially cook it.

2. Then, take out the biscuit dough and divide it into equal pieces that can be wrapped around the hot dog.

3. Take each hot dog and wrap it in a piece of cheese with some pickle and wrap it in the biscuit dough.

4. Then, take the cheese corn dogs and roast them over the fire so that the dough becomes fully cooked and the cheese melts.

46. Marinated Salmon:

Serves: 4

Cooking time: 10 minutes

Ingredients:

- Salmon

- 1 minced garlic clove

- Salt and black pepper

- ½ cup of lemon juice, freshly squeezed

- Half an onion, diced

- ¼ cup of olive oil

- 2 teaspoons dill powder

Directions:

1. If you have pre-prepared your marinade and it is frozen, make sure to thaw it. Then, place your salmon into a shallow dish and allow it to marinate for 20

minutes before taking it out. You may dispose of the remainder of the marinade.

2. Place the fish on the grill with the skin side being on the grill. Cook it for about 10 to 15 minutes or until the fish skin becomes flaky and changes color to become white.

47.Cheesy Beef Burgers

Serves: 2

Cooking time: 10 minutes

Ingredients:

- 1 teaspoon black pepper

- 2 to 3 tablespoons of vegetable oil

- 1 ½ pounds of lean ground beef

- 1 teaspoon salt

- 4 hamburger buns

- ¼ cup parmesan

Toppings

- 5 mozzarella cheese slices

- 1 large tomatoes, sliced

- 4 basil leaves, chopped

- 1 bunch of parsley, chopped

Directions:

1. Place the salt, pepper, beef, and cheese in a dish. Then, combine each of these ingredients to form four burgers. Create an indentation in the center of the patty by pressing your thumb there to enable it to cook thoroughly.

2. Apply some vegetable oil to the grill and then place the burgers on the grill over the barbecue. Cook each side for about five minutes before flipping. Then, add a bit of cheese on top of the patty before removing from the grill.

3. Place the patties onto the burger buns and allow them to grill.

4. Add the desired toppings, including the parsley, basil and onion.

5. Serve while hot.

48.Chicken and Vegetable Foil Packets:

Serves: 4

Cooking time: 40 minutes

Ingredients:

- 450 grams of cubed chicken breast

- 6 to 8 mushrooms

- 1 diced onion

- ¼ cup butter

- 4 cubed small potatoes

- Juice of one lemon

- 3 diced garlic cloves

Directions:

1. Place the potatoes, onion, chicken, mushrooms and garlic in a sealable bag or container. Then, add the lemon juice and mix together evenly. Divide the chicken and vegetables into four different aluminum

foil pockets. Add some butter and seal each of the pockets.

2.   Insert the aluminum foil packets onto a barbecue or campfire grill and allow them to cook for 35 minutes or longer until the chicken and potatoes are cooked. Once it is done, take the pockets out of the fire and allow them to cool. After leaving it, carefully open it to refrain from getting burned by the steam encapsulated in the packets.

49. Rosemary Chicken and Potato

Serves: 4

Cooking time: 10-20 minutes

Ingredients:

- 8 chicken thighs

- 20 fingerling potatoes

- Vegetable oil

- ½ teaspoon each of salt, paprika and black pepper

- ½ cup BBQ sauce

- 1 can beer

- A few sprigs of rosemary

Directions:

1. Put the paprika, salt, pepper, soda, BBQ sauce and chicken thighs in a sealable container. Mix thoroughly and leave to marinate for 45 minutes.

2. Mix together some salt and rosemary with vegetable oil and then coat the potatoes after cutting them in half.

3. Set up the fire and until there are no more flames and only hot coals remain. Then, place the chicken and potatoes on the oiled vegetable grill and wait for them to cook. This takes about 25 to 35 minutes.

4. Check that they are fully cooked through and that the chicken is not raw. Leave the meat to rest for a bit before serving.

50. Orange-Flavored Chicken Wings

Serves: 6

Cooking time: 30 minutes

Ingredients:

- ½ teaspoon red pepper powder and black pepper powder each

- ½ cup of soy sauce

- 1 kg of chicken wings

- ¼ cup of orange juice

- ¼ cup of honey

- 1 tablespoon of grated ginger

Directions:

1. Combine the red pepper, soy sauce, orange juice, ginger and black pepper together in a bowl. Coat the chicken with the marinade and leave it for an hour.

2. Prepare the barbecue and cook the wings for 20 minutes on the grill, rotating them once or twice to ensure they are evenly cooked.

3. Mix the sugar with the remaining soy sauce and pour over the wings. Serve them with carrot or celery sticks.

Conclusion:

Part of the beauty of eating outdoors while camping is that things that are grilled taste quite delicious due to their simplicity. A piece of steak or a kebab that is roasted over a fire is often flavorful and succulent, making mealtimes truly tantalizing for experienced campers. Even if you haven't brought with you a couple of juicy steaks, you can always roast or grill a fish you caught in the nearby lake over the fire and enjoy your meal. You'll find that tasting something you caught with your own two hands tastes better than something you bought and stored in your cooler.

Either way, however, you are sure to like any meal you make over a campfire if you follow the recipes in this book. If you need any inspiration, flip through this cookbook to find a recipe that you find really appealing and make sure to bring with you any ingredients that you cannot find in nature! There are so many delicious recipes you can appreciate while cooking outdoors, so as long as you have with you a few basic tools or cooking equipment, you will be able to prep the most fantastic dishes over your campfire. We promise you that the recipes included therein will make your mouth water!

CPSIA information can be obtained
at www.ICGtesting.com
Printed in the USA
BVHW042330160521
607527BV00014B/598